NATIVE AMERICAN LEGENDS
CHIEF JOSEPH

Don McLeese

Rourke
Publishing LLC
Vero Beach, Florida 32964

www.rourkepublishing.com

PHOTO CREDITS:
©Hulton/Archive by Getty Images pg 5
©Smithsonian Institution, Bureau of American Ethnology Cover
©Library of Congress all other photos

Title page: *Portrait of Chief Joseph when he was a young man*

Editor: Frank Sloan

Cover and page design by Nicola Stratford

Library of Congress Cataloging-in-Publication Data

McLeese, Don.
  Chief Joseph / Don McLeese.
    p. cm. -- (Native American legends)
Summary: A brief biography of the famous Nez Perce leader who led his people against the United States Army and lost, but won the respect of his own people as well as white generals by standing up for his beliefs.

Includes bibliographical references and index.
  ISBN 1-58952-726-7 (hardcover)
  1. Joseph, Nez Perce Chief, 1840-1904--Juvenile literature. 2. Nez Perce Indians--Kings and rulers--Biography--Juvenile literature. 3. Nez Perce Indians--Wars, 1877--Juvenile literature. [1. Joseph, Nez Perce Chief, 1840-1904. 2. Nez Perce Indians--Biography. 3. Indians of North America--Biography. 4. Kings, queens, rulers, etc.] I. Title. II. Series.
  E99.N5J653 2003
  979.5004'9741--dc21

                                                2003004371

Printed in the USA
w/w

Table of Contents

A Famous Chief

The **Native American** known as **Chief** Joseph became famous throughout the country in the 1870s. He was considered a great leader not only by Native Americans, but by the white **settlers** who had taken land from the Native Americans for the United States. Chief Joseph said it was wrong for the United States to take the land. He said that his people of the **Nez Perce tribe** should live where they had always lived, in what is now northeast Oregon and Idaho.

Chief Joseph tried hard to keep his tribe free to live where they wanted. He said the United States had no right to keep his people on a **reservation**.

The United States won and Chief Joseph lost, but he never changed his mind. He knew he was right and the country was wrong. He was called the **conscience** of his people because he stood up for what he believed.

A full-length photograph of Chief Joseph

Joseph the Younger

The baby who would grow up to be Chief Joseph was born in 1840. His tribe lived in the Wallowa Valley, in what is now the northeast part of Oregon. His father was also known as Joseph, and he was the chief of the Nez Perce tribe.

Father Joseph had taken that name after becoming a member of the **Christian** religion. This was the religion of many of the white settlers. Some Native Americans believed that if they became Christians, they and the white settlers could live in peace.

Christian Religion
When white settlers came to this country, they brought the Christian religion with them. This religion says that Jesus Christ was the son of God. Some Native Americans started to believe this as well.

When Chief Joseph was a boy, his name was pronounced Hin-mah-too-yah-lat-kekt. In the Native American language, this meant "Thunder Rolling Down the Mountain." But many in the tribe called him Joseph, after his father. They called the father Joseph the **Elder** and the son Joseph the Younger, so everyone would know the difference.

A typical Nez Perce infant shown in a cradleboard

Peaceful Tribe

The Nez Perce tribe was known as peaceful. It didn't want to fight the white people coming into the territory. When a number of white people came to explore the land as part of the Lewis and Clark **expedition**, the Nez Perce made friends with them. Joseph the Elder even helped the United States set up a reservation where the tribe could live. In 1855, the tribe and the country agreed that a long stretch of land that went from Oregon into Idaho would be the reservation where the Nez Perce would live.

Lewis and Clark Expedition
In 1804, President Thomas Jefferson asked two men, Meriwether Lewis and William Clark, to lead a trip west to see what was on this new land that the United States had bought.

Lewis and Clark hold a meeting with friendly Indians.

Gold Rush

In the early 1860s, gold was found in the land belonging to the Nez Perce, and a number of white settlers came to try to find more. Gold was worth a lot of money, so much that people would leave where they lived and rush to the land where it was found. This was called a "gold rush."

Though the United States had promised this land to the Nez Perce, the country broke its promise once gold was found there. The country said the tribe would have to stay on a much smaller piece of land. This new reservation was in Idaho, a long way from the land in Oregon that was home to Joseph the Elder and Joseph the Younger.

Reservations
Native Americans had long believed that land belongs to everyone and that no one can own it. They didn't like it when the United States said the tribes had to stay on a reservation.

◄ *An old colored engraving shows a wagon train in the Platte Valley during the years of the gold rush.*

A Promise Is Broken

When the United States broke its promise, this made Joseph the Elder very angry. He had trusted the white settlers. He had even become a Christian like them, believing in their religion. But the United States had lied to him. The country wanted him to sign a **treaty**, which was a paper that said he agreed to the new reservation. Joseph the Elder said he wouldn't sign it, and he wouldn't move his people to Idaho.

◄ *A photograph showing U.S. soldiers overlooking an encampment of tipis*

A New Chief

Joseph the Elder died in 1871, and his tribe needed to choose a new chief. It chose his son, Joseph the Younger. From then on, the son was known simply as Chief Joseph. He believed like his father had that the country had no right to make the Nez Perce leave their land. Even when a lot more white settlers came looking for gold, Chief Joseph and his people refused to move to Idaho.

A painting of Chief Joseph done by E.A. Burbank ➤

CHIEF JOSEPH.
NEZ PERCES.

The Government Changes Its Mind

In 1873, the United States issued an order saying that the Wallowa Valley belonged to the tribe and that the white settlers should leave. This made Chief Joseph very happy, because he knew that his people belonged on this land. But then the government changed its mind again. It said the Nez Perce must leave their home for the reservation in Idaho.

In 1877, General Oliver Otis Howard was told by the government to attack Chief Joseph's people if they would not move. Chief Joseph was a peaceful man, and he knew that the soldiers would kill his people if they didn't move. So he started leading his tribe toward Idaho.

A photograph of General Howard ➤

General Oliver Otis Howard
Howard later wrote many books about Native Americans, including *Famous Indian Chiefs I Have Known.*

Killing White Settlers

Some of the tribe's younger **warriors** became very angry at having to move. About 20 of them attacked white settlers who were living nearby and killed several of them. The U.S. Army was told to make sure the Native Americans moved to the reservation and to kill them if they didn't.

Many of the Native Americans wanted to fight the army. Chief Joseph didn't want to fight, but he didn't want to move all the way to the reservation, either. Instead, he led his people to move away from the soldiers and to fight them when they needed to.

A group of drawings that show scenes from the Nez Perce war. *The picture first appeared in* Harper's Weekly *in 1877.*

GEORGE A. HUSTON, GUIDE.

SOUNDING THE BUGLE FOR THE TRUCE.

SENDING FLAG OF TRUCE TO THE INDIAN CAMP.

THE BATTLE — ADVANCE OF THE SKIRMISH LINE.

Chief Joseph showed both the Native Americans and the generals leading the fight against them that he was a great leader, as he moved his people on a 1,400-mile (2,253-kilometer) march. Over three months during the summer of 1877, there were four big battles. Chief Joseph only had about 200 warriors in his band of 700 Native Americans. The army had 2,000 soldiers, ten times as many fighters as were in the tribe.

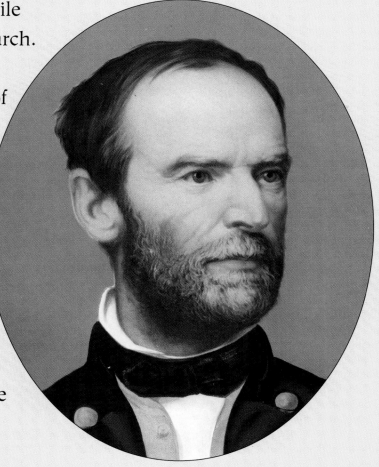

Even so, General William Tecumseh Sherman praised Chief Joseph and his warriors for their "courage and skill." They made the most of the few warriors they had, surprising the army. The Native Americans didn't beat the army in battle, but the army didn't beat the Native Americans either.

General William Tecumseh Sherman Sherman had become one of the most famous American generals during the Civil War of 1861-65.

◄ A photo of General Sherman taken around the time of the battles with Chief Joseph

Surrender

On October 5, 1877, Chief Joseph told his warriors to stop fighting and surrender to the United States. The army had too many soldiers and too many weapons for the Native Americans to keep going.

Even though his tribe lost, Chief Joseph had made a great fight and had won the respect of the white generals. Chief Joseph became famous throughout the United States as one of the greatest leaders of Native Americans.

An illustration that appeared in Frank Leslie's ➤
Illustrated Newspaper *in 1877. It shows General Miles charging an Indian camp.*

Back Toward Home

Chief Joseph continued to believe that the Native Americans should be allowed to return where they'd lived instead of staying on the reservation in Idaho. He even went to Washington, D.C., in 1879 to ask President Rutherford B. Hayes about this.

In 1885, the Native Americans were allowed to leave Idaho and go west. But Chief Joseph didn't get to go home to what is now Oregon. Instead, the government made him go to another tribe's reservation in what is now northern Washington.

An official photograph of President Hayes

President Rutherford B. Hayes
Hayes had been governor of Ohio before he won a very close election in 1876 to become president.

A Broken Heart

Chief Joseph died in 1904. His doctor said it was because of "a broken heart." Chief Joseph felt bad because he was homesick, and his people couldn't live where they wanted. He knew that the United States had treated his people badly. He said, "If the white man wants to live in peace with the Indian, he can. Treat all men alike. Give them a chance to live and grow." All he'd wanted was for the United States to treat his people fairly.

A photograph of Chief Joseph in his traditional war bonnet, made of feathers and beads ➤

Chief Joseph's People

The name Nez Perce means "pierced nose" in French. These Native Americans fed themselves by hunting, fishing, and eating plants. The Nez Perce were good horse breeders and bred the first Appaloosa horses.

The United States took the land where the Nez Perce had been able to move around. They said the Nez Perce must stay on a smaller piece of land known as a reservation.

In the early 1800s there were about 6,000 Nez Perce. Because of war and disease, the number dropped, and today there are about 3,000 Nez Perce left.

Time Line

1840 — Chief Joseph (the Younger) is born.

1855 — Joseph the Elder agrees to move his tribe to a reservation.

1860s — Gold Rush.

1871 — Joseph the Elder dies, and Joseph the Younger becomes chief.

1873 — The United States says Wallowa Valley belongs to Native Americans.

1877 — Chief Joseph leads his tribe in a brave fight against U.S. soldiers.

1879 — Chief Joseph goes to Washington, D.C.

1885 — Native Americans leave Idaho to return west.

1904 — Chief Joseph dies.

Glossary

chief (CHEEF) — leader, head of a Native American tribe

Christian (KRIS chun) — a religion that believes that Jesus Christ is the son of God

conscience (CAHN shunce) — the part of a person that knows the difference between right and wrong

elder (ELL dur) — older

expedition (ecks peh DIH shun) — a trip to explore, or a journey with some other purpose

Native Americans (NAY tiv uh MARE ih canz) — those who lived in the land that is now the United States before explorers from Europe came

Nez Perce (nehz PURS or nehz pur SAY) — a tribe of Native Americans that lived in what is now Idaho and Oregon

reservation (rehz ur VAY shun) — land where Native Americans were told they had to live

settlers (SET lurz) — people who move to a new land to live there

treaty (TREE tee) — a paper that people sign that says they agree to something

tribe (TRYB) — one of the bands or nations of Native Americans

warriors (WAHR ee urz) — great fighters in battle

Further Reading

McAuliffe, Bill. *Chief Joseph of the Nez Perce: A Photo-Illustrated Biography.* Bridgestone Books, 1997

Noyed, Robert B. *Chief Joseph: Chief of the Nez Perce.* Child's World, 2002

Taylor, Marian W. *Chief Joseph: Nez Perce Leader.* Chelsea House Publishing, 1993

Websites to Visit

www.pbs.org/weta/thewest/people/a_c/chiefjoseph.htm

www.indians.org/welker/joseph.htm

www.powersource.com/gallery/people/joseph.html

Index

About The Author

Don McLeese is an award-winning journalist whose work has appeared in many newspapers and magazines. He earned his M.A. degree in English from the University of Chicago, taught feature writing at the University of Texas and has frequently contributed to the World Book Encyclopedia. He lives with his wife and two daughters in West Des Moines, Iowa.